AN UNOFFICIAL ROBLOX BOOK

DIARY OF A
ROBLOX
PRO

ZOMBIE INVASION

SCHOLASTIC

Published in the UK by Scholastic, 2023
Scholastic, Bosworth Avenue, Warwick, CV34 6UQ
Scholastic Ireland, 89E Lagan Road, Dublin Industrial Estate, Glasnevin, Dublin, D11 HP5F

First published in Australia by Scholastic Australia Pty Limited, 2023

Text © Scholastic Australia, 2023
Cover and inside illustrations © Scholastic Australia, 2023
Cover design by Hannah Janzen
Internal design by Paul Hallam

ISBN 978 0702 32937 1

A CIP catalogue record for this book is available from the British Library.

Printed in the UK
Paper made from wood grown in sustainable forests and other controlled sources.

MIX
Paper | Supporting
responsible forestry
FSC® C018072
FSC
www.fsc.org

3 5 7 9 10 8 6 4

This is a work of fiction. Any resemblance to actual people, events or locales is entirely coincidental.

www.scholastic.co.uk

For safety or quality concerns:
UK: www.scholastic.co.uk/productinformation
EU: www.scholastic.ie/productinformation

MONDAY AFTERNOON

'You're about to get bloxxed!'
I said, **PUNCHING** away at
my controller.

'Not if I get you first, Ari!' Zeke
turned his avatar on the screen

to face me. A spray of laser bullets came firing out of his super blaster on the game.

I ducked.

'Ha-ha, missed!' I yelled.

Suddenly, there was an epic **BOOM** on screen and the head of my zombie avatar went flying off my shoulders. This was quickly followed by Zeke's avatar's legs falling off and his zombie collapsing into a heap of **GREEN GOO.**

'Hey, what the—?!' I squealed in protest.

'BLOXXED,' Jez said with a laugh.

Jez's zombie hunter avatar stood triumphantly on the screen with the words **WINNER** flashing over her head. She'd blasted Zeke and me (who were the zombies) to pieces and had won the game.

'Bruh, you *always* win when you're the **ZOMBIE HUNTER,'** I whined. 'How do you do it?'

'Pure skill,' Jez said, her eyebrows raised.

'Rematch?' Zeke challenged.

'Nah, I'm done,' Jez said, throwing the controller to the floor.

'I'll play you, Zeke—one more round then I've gotta go,' I said, resetting the game.

Jez opened her laptop and started flicking through all her systems. Jez was a **TECH WHIZ** and the best hacker I knew. She had all these trackers on different systems—she tracked **SECRET PORTALS,** army databases and even the school computers. She never liked to be away from her laptop for too long in case there was something interesting happening online.

Without Jez playing as the zombie hunter, Zeke and I were able to blitz the field of other zombies until there was only the two of us left. We now had to race to get to the final checkpoint before sunrise, at which time we'd melt into a puddle of **OOZY** green liquid and it'd be game over.

Meanwhile, Jez was **TAPPING** away on her keyboard.

A head poked around the corner of the doorway. 'Hey, Jez!' Jez's little brother, Max, was looking at her with wide eyes. But he got no response.

'Jez!' he repeated.

Jez kept tapping, oblivious.

'JEZ!'

'Huh? What is it, Max?' Jez said, annoyed that he'd interrupted her.

'Mum said you and your friends can have some cookies,' he said, proudly holding up a chocolate-chip **COOKIE.** 'We made them this afternoon.'

'Ah, no thanks,' Jez said, waving her hand dismissively.

Max looked down, disappointed.

'I'd love to try one, Max,' I said.

Max looked up excitedly then
DARTED back off to the
kitchen to grab more of his cookies
for us.

'Me too, Max!' Zeke called
after him.

'He's so **ANNOYING,'**
Jez mumbled.

'He's funny!' I said. 'You're too
mean to him,' I joked.

Jez rolled her eyes. 'You wouldn't be saying that if it was your sister, Ally.'

Jez was right. But Ally wasn't funny like Max. She was totally annoying.

Max **BOUNDED** back in with a bowl of cookies. He held it out to Zeke and me and we took one each. He offered one again to Jez, but she waved him away with her hand again.

Max stood, watching, waiting for us to take a bite.

'Wow, these are great, Max!'
I said as I chewed the slightly
overcooked cookie.

'PRO BAKER!' Zeke added.

Max beamed.

'You can go now,' Jez said without
looking up.

Max's face fell as he walked out
of the room.

'Maybe we should let Max play?'
I offered.

'No point,' Jez said flatly. 'He **HATES** gaming.'

'**OH.**'

'And computers and coding and hacking and everything else cool,' she added. 'We have absolutely **NOTHING** in common.'

I turned back to my game right as Zeke blasted my zombie head off. It went **FLYING** across the screen and landed in the river, then bobbed away with the current.

'BLOXXED!' Zeke yelled.

I threw a cushion at him and he threw it back, laughing.

'WHOA,' Jez breathed as something chimed on her computer.

'What is it?' Zeke said, leaning in closer.

I crawled around behind Jez and peered over too. She had an app open labelled **'PORTAL TRACKER'.**

'Not this again,' I complained.

'No, look,' she said. 'I think I've found one.'

Jez was obsessed with finding a portal to **ANOTHER DIMENSION.** I still wasn't sure portals existed, but Zeke's dad was in the army and he said they tracked them all the time. But portals rarely just showed up in a town like Blockville.

'Look here,' Jez said, pointing to a map that had a **RADAR** on it. There were different colours shaded across the screen, and at one point there was a **BLINKING RED DOT** above a cloud of swirling purple pixels. 'This is definite portal activity,' she said.

'Where?' I asked, leaning closer.

She pointed to an area on the map that was on the outskirts of town. I knew the place well— it was an **ABANDONED** industrial complex and we'd been there before. We'd almost been captured by a **MONSTER** there, but after we escaped, the monster disappeared. Sometimes I'd wonder if it even happened at all, or if it were just a dream.

'I'm not going back to that
CREEPY PLACE,' I said,
shaking my head.

'But this could be our chance.
Imagine if there really was
a portal!' she said breathlessly.

'Yeah, and now imagine what
might come out of that portal,'
I said, eyebrows raised.

'But how often do we get to track
a **REAL PORTAL?** It's too
good to refuse,' Jez pleaded.

We both looked at Zeke. 'OK, I admit, it's pretty cool. Maybe we could go just to check it out. You know, on the **DOWN LOW,'** he said.

'Well, it's getting dark and I have to go home,' I said, glancing at the clock on the wall.

'We can go tomorrow afternoon!' Jez said. 'According to Portal Tracker, this portal is still forming. It won't even be open yet. We have time.'

'I'm in,' said Zeke, smiling.

'Fine,' I said.

'YEEESSSSS!' Jez cheered.

'Where are we going?' a voice said from the doorway.

'*We* are not going anywhere, Max,' Jez said, standing up and gently pushing her little brother back through the doorway. 'And you need to stop spying on me.'

'You never let me have any fun with you!' Max said, tears filling his eyes. Then he ran off to his room.

'Little **SNEAK,**' Jez muttered. 'So, tomorrow? After school?'

'OK,' Zeke and I said in unison.

I gathered my stuff and said thanks to Jez's mum for having me over. Then I headed out the door to walk home.

As I walked the quiet streets of **BLOCKVILLE,** my mind started going wild with thoughts about all the things that could be in the portal. What if there was another monster but we couldn't **ESCAPE** this time?

Or what if it took us to another Block World and we became trapped? And while I like the idea of not having to do homework or chores ever again, I'd miss Coda too much.

TUESDAY LUNCHTIME

'Ready for some **PORTAL HUNTING** this afternoon?'
Jez asked excitedly before taking a huge bite of her toasted sandwich.

'Yeah, yeah,' I sighed. I was getting a bit bored with her portal **OBSESSION.**

'Who's going portal hunting?' a little voice squeaked from behind us.

'Hi, Gabe,' Zeke said, as they high-fived.

Gabe was the smartest little avatar at school. He was put up two years ahead of his age, so he was often bullied for being a bit of a **NERD.** But we'd gotten to know him better, and turns out he was a **COOL GUY.**

'Take a seat,' I said, shifting along the bench to make more room.

'I'm on my way to the library,' he said, pushing his glasses up his nose. 'I'm meeting Gus, the **ΠΕШ ΚΙΔ,** there.'

'Good for you,' I said. The new kid was a lot like Gabe—really into studying and science and stuff. It was nice that he'd finally found a good friend.

'But what were you saying about portal hunting?' he asked.

'I think I've tracked a portal to the industrial area on the outskirts of town,' Jez said proudly.

'We're gonna go check it out later.'

'**WHOA,** be careful,' Gabe said. 'You never know what might come out of one of those!'

'Like what?' I said, a slight **QUIVER** in my voice. Ever since we'd been chased by a monster in the warehouse, I was not so keen on meeting weird creatures.

'I dunno. Monsters, pirates, **ZOMBIES,**' Gabe said.

'Zombies?' Zeke said. 'Cool!'

'Not really!' Gabe laughed. 'You know they, like, **EAT YOUR BRAINS** and stuff. And if one of them touches you, you turn into a zombie. too.'

I swallowed hard.

'You can turn back though, right?' I said.

'Not unless you blast the **BOSS ZOMBIE,**' Gabe said.

'Boss zombie?' Zeke asked.

'Yeah—like their leader. If you

defeat it, the zombie infection leaves you and you turn back. But it has to happen within, like, a few hours, otherwise you are a **ZOMBIE FOR LIFE.** I've read about it online,' Gabe exlained.

'How do you defeat a zombie when it's already dead?!' I asked.

Gabe shrugged. 'Good luck!' He walked off towards the library.

'Man, if something creepy comes out of that portal, I am OUT of there,' I said.

'Yeah, deal,' Jez agreed. 'I want to investigate, but I'm not so happy to be monster dinner or zombie breakfast.'

'I'll bring snacks!' Zeke said happily.

'Snacks?! How can you think of snacks when we're talking about monsters and zombies?!' I said.

Zeke shrugged. He was either **SUPER BRAVE** or he didn't believe anything was coming out of that portal.

'Well, we'll see this afternoon,

I guess,' Jez said. 'But, is it OK
if we go by my house first?
I promised mum I would walk Max
home before we go explore.' She
rolled her eyes.

'Naw, be nice to the little guy,'
I said, defending Max.

'Yeah, well, we're dropping him
home. He's not coming with us,' Jez
said firmly.

I had to agree. If there really
were monsters coming out of that
portal, it would be no place for
a **LITTLE AVATAR.**

Part of me was excited to go, but the other part was a bit nervous. There was no way I wanted to face the hairy monster in that industrial compound again.

TUESDAY AFTER SCHOOL

'And then I ran up the wing
and **STOLE** the ball . . .'

'Uh-huh.'

'And I **DRIBBLED** it up
the sideline . . .'

'Uh-huh.'

'Then I took this **EPIC KICK**
and the ball sailed through the
air . . .'

'Uh-huh.'

'And it bounced off the crossbar!
But I took the **REBOUND** . . .'

'Uh-huh.'

'And I took another kick and the
ball went straight into the goal!
And we **WON!**'

'Uh-huh.'

Max stopped walking and
frowned. We all turned to look
at him. 'Jez, you aren't even
listening to my story!'

'Uh-huh,' Jez replied, proving
his point.

'I was listening, Max. It sounded
EPIC!' I said.

Max smiled, but I could tell he
was still hurt by Jez's behaviour.

'Sorry, Max, we just have other
things on our minds right now,'
Zeke said. 'We're going to check
out a portal and—'

'A **PORTAL?!**' Max shrieked.

'Zeke! Why'd you tell him?!' Jez

hissed. 'Now he's going to want
to come!'

'Can I?' Max asked with hopeful
eyes.

'No,' Jez replied. 'You're too little
and you'll just get in the way.'

Max's shoulders **DROOPED.**

'Maybe next time?' I offered.

We reached Jez's house and
went in through the gate. Max
stomped up to the front door
and opened it.

'See you later, Max!' I called.

Max turned back and scowled at Jez, then he walked through the door and **SLAMMED** it closed behind him.

'Little dude seems upset,' I said.

'Whatever,' Jez dismissed. 'He has tantrums all the time. He'll get over it. Let's go!'

I felt bad about hurting Max's feelings, but my mind quickly returned to the industrial compound. We dumped our

schoolbags on Jez's doorstep,
but Zeke kept his on his back.

'Leave your bag, Zeke,' Jez said.

'Nah—I've got . . . supplies.' He
winked.

I knew what that meant. **FOOD.**
Zeke was always thinking about
his stomach and never went
anywhere without snacks.

We walked for what seemed like
HOURS before getting to the
outskirts of town. The houses
became more spread out and the

shops were either rundown or completely **ABANDONED.**

We finally made it to the compound and it looked exactly the same as it had the last time we were here.

We climbed the fence into the compound and looked around. It was completely silent except for the sound of a gentle breeze blowing dust around our feet. Jez **COUGHED** slightly.

Just beyond from where we stood was an old petrol station I didn't remember seeing last time. It was surrounded by a tall security fence with several **NO TRESPASSING** signs, and a small section of the fence had been detached and pushed inwards, like a makeshift gate. It looked like a good hiding spot if we were in danger.

'Where's the portal?' Zeke asked.

Jez pulled her phone out of her pocket and opened the tracking app. Zeke and I looked on, even though we really had no idea what all the green circles and flashing red lights meant.

'I think this way,' Jez said, pointing further into the complex.

We walked nervously through the abandoned dirt streets. It was **EERILY QUIET.**

Zeke started riffling through his backpack and pulled out a bag of chips. 'Snack?' he asked, offering it to us.

Jez shook her head.

'How can you think about food at a time like this?' I said, also refusing the offer. My stomach was too full of butterflies to be hungry.

'Drink, then?' he said, opening his backpack and showing us the inside. There were several bottles of **LEMONADE.**

'When'd you have time to get so many snacks?' Jez asked.

'Bought them at the corner store

while you were getting Max
from his classroom,' Zeke said,
shrugging. 'Want one?'

'No, thanks,' Jez and I said at the
same time.

Jez's app started **BEEPING.**
I looked at her with wide eyes.

'This way,' she whispered.

We walked past a pile of old tyres
and a mountain of twisted metal
and junk. The same burnt-out
car from last time was still here,
and there was a broken shopping

trolley lying upside down.

We stopped outside a particularly dilapidated old building and Jez turned her head from side to side, taking everything in.

'Do you—' I began.

'SHH!' she hissed.

Her phone beeped louder.

I heard a rustle behind us. We all turned in alarm. There was a light clang as something touched the metal of a big barrel sitting

outside the building. The barrel
WOBBLED.

'What is it?' I whispered, my knees quivering.

'The portal?!' Zeke breathed.

We tiptoed over to the barrel. The barrels were small, so whatever was behind it couldn't have been *too* big.

'On the count of three, move the barrel,' Jez whispered.

'Are you sure?!' I asked.

'There are three of us. We'll be stronger than whatever is behind it,' Zeke said.

I nodded.

'One . . .

Two . . .

THREE!'

TUESDAY AFTERNOON— A BIT LATER

Zeke did a flying parkour kick, sending the barrel toppling over.

'**AAAAAAGGGH!**' something screamed.

'**AAAAAAGGGGH!**' we all screamed.

'Max!' Jez yelled angrily.

Her little brother was crouched
behind the barrel, looking terrified.
He was wearing a baseball cap
pulled down over his eyes.

'What are you *doing* here?!'
she demanded.

'I—I just wanted to come too,'
he stammered.

'You followed us?' Zeke asked.

'I just wanted to see the portal. I brought some things that could help,' he added quickly, trying to open his backpack to show us.

But Jez didn't want to see whatever toys he'd brought along. 'Max, you are such a **PAIN!**' she said angrily, shoving his bag aside.

Max's little eyes filled with tears.

'And now we have to look after you so you don't get lost,' she said, slapping her forehead.

Max looked down at his feet. Zeke and I stood in awkward silence as tears dripped from Max's eyes and Jez frowned, furious.

But before we could say anything, a cold wind suddenly whipped through the compound. The wheels on the abandoned trolley spun fast, **SQUEAKING** as they turned. The sky went dark as a huge rain cloud blew in from nowhere. Most frightening of all was the **EERIE** purple light that emanated from behind the building we were standing next to.

'What's going on?' I said shakily.

We stalked along the building and
rounded the corner to see where
the light was coming from. And
when we got there, we couldn't
believe our eyes.

TUESDAY AFTERNOON— EVEN LATER

'WHOA!' we all breathed in unison.

Max trembled and moved in closer to Jez. Jez didn't look so angry anymore and she let him snuggle into her side.

We all stared at the huge beam of purple light, which swirled around in a tornado shape.

'Is that . . .' I started.

'A portal,' Jez breathed.

None of us had ever seen one
IRL. It was beautiful and scary
and **OMINOUS** all at the
same time.

'We should get out of here,'
I said after we'd had a good look.
'Imagine if we got sucked into it.'

'I'm with Ari,' Zeke said. 'I think this is too **RISKY**. We've seen it, now let's go.'

'Just another minute,' Jez said, taking a small step towards the portal. 'I just want to see if I can look **INSIDE**.'

She took another step forward. Max was still clinging to her T-shirt and walked towards it with her.

Jez leaned in.

'Not so close, Jez!' I warned.

'Max, maybe you should come back here,' Zeke said, worried about the little avatar.

'I can almost see . . .' Jez said, stepping closer. Her hair whipped around her face as the tornado of light spun faster and faster, casting a purple haze across the dry earth.

'Jez . . .' I said.

Suddenly, a long green arm reached out of the portal. It **GRABBED** Max by the T-shirt and pulled. Jez reached for her brother, but the green arm was too strong. Max was halfway into the portal.

'Jez!' Max screamed.

'MAX!' Jez yelled. She lunged forward to try to grab her brother, but the creature leaned all the way out of the portal to push her back. The avatar had a green head with vacant, **DEAD EYES** that stared straight into Jez. His ragged clothes hung off his body and his wrinkly skin looked like scrunched-up old paper. His wonky teeth hung loosely from his mouth as he groaned. Then he yelled one terrifying word.

'ZOMBIE!' we all screeched at the top of our lungs.

Max disappeared into the portal and Jez tumbled backwards.

Max's bag was flung off his shoulders and landed at my feet.

'Let's get out of here!' Zeke **SHRIEKED.**

'But . . . Max!' Jez cried.

I picked up the backpack and pulled Jez away from the portal so she wouldn't get sucked in herself. Then we ran around to the other side of the building and hid behind the old car wreck.

'Max!' she **BLUBBERED** as fresh tears spilled from her eyes.

'Jez, listen!' I said, getting her to focus on me. 'We can get Max back, but we need a strategy. We can't just run into the portal.'

Jez nodded, wiping the tears from her cheeks and frowning with **DETERMINATION.** 'OK. What do we do?'

We had to think of a **PLAN.** And fast.

TUESDAY AFTERNOON— MUCH LATER

'The zombies are probably going to come out of the portal. Why else would they be here?' I said, thinking aloud.

'And we all know what zombies like to eat,' Zeke added with a shudder. **'BRAINS!** And there aren't any brains in this abandoned place aside from us.'

'Which means they're going to

come out and **INVADE** our town,' I predicted. 'We need to be ready for when they do.'

'What about Max?' Jez said.

'The zombies may have turned him into one already, so he'll probably be with them when they attack,' I said.

'Max is a zombie?!' Jez screamed.

'Remember what Gabe said,' I reminded her. 'We have to get the **BOSS ZOMBIE** and then Max will be back to normal.'

Jez nodded.

'What have we got?' I said, opening up Max's bag to see if there was anything helpful in it.

Zeke opened his own bag, but all he had was food and lemonade.

I reached into Max's bag and pulled out three **WATER BLASTERS.**

'They're just toys,' I said, disappointed. We couldn't blast away zombies with a toy.

'Anything else?' Jez said, looking in.

I shook my head. OK, so Max's stuff wasn't going to help. We'd have to think of something else.

The sun began to dip low, hiding itself behind the dark, **MOODY CLOUDS.** It was almost like it was night-time. Which was usually when . . .

A deep, rumbling noise sounded

from behind the building. I noticed the glowing purple light had intensified. And that's when we heard a droning sound . . .

TUESDAY— LATE AFTERNOON

'BRAAAAAIIIINNNNS!'

We tiptoed to the side of the
building and peeked our heads
around the corner to see the portal.

AAAAAGHHHHH! I internally
screamed.

Out of the portal spilled what
looked like twenty zombies. One by

one, they piled out of the opening,
dragging their hanging limbs
behind them. Their vacant eyes
stared into the distance as they
groaned a monstrous chorus.

One of them sniffed the air,
then pointed in our direction.
'Avataaaaaaars!' he moaned.

The other zombies turned and
began limping towards us.

AAAAAAAGGGGH!

'Wait, look!' Zeke said, pointing
to the mob of zombies.

In the front row was a little
zombie wearing a black
BASEBALL CAP.

'It's Max!' Zeke yelled.

'MAX!' Jez screeched
as she began to run
towards her zombie
brother. But Max
didn't recognise her.
His empty eyes
stared past her.

I grabbed Jez's arm, pulling her
back. 'Jez, no! He isn't himself. If
you go over there, you'll become

a zombie too, and that isn't going
to help Max, is it?'

Jez shook her head.

'The only way to **DEFEAT**
these things is to find the boss
zombie and get rid of him. That
will turn Max back. And without
their leader, I reckon the other
zombies will return to the portal.'

'Come on,' Zeke said, pointing
towards the fence surrounding the
compound. 'They'll be heading to
the gate to get to town. We need
to cut them off.'

We turned and saw that one half of the **ZOMBIE MOB** were heading around to the other side of the building. They were surrounding us. We had to **MOVE!**

TUESDAY— EVEN LATER

We bolted through the abandoned dirt streets towards where we entered at the front of the compound.

'We need to stop the zombies from leaving here in order to save the town,' I said.

'But this fence is only shoulder height. They're going to be able to get out just as easily as we got in,' Zeke said.

'We'll need to block it off. Or contain them somehow,' I said, thinking aloud. 'I don't know if zombies can climb, but they're pretty slow. If we can **TRAP** them somewhere inside the compound, it would take them forever to get over the outer fence.'

I looked around. The fence was the same height the whole way around, we definitely wouldn't be able to block it all at once.

We could hear the monstrous **GROANS** of the zombie mob

get louder as they slowly made
their way up the street towards us.

I turned to my left and saw
it— the abandoned **PETROL
STATION.** The periphery of
the station was cordoned off with
a mesh security fence that looked
a lot taller and sturdier than the
one surrounding the compound. The
petrol station had several pumps,
a little pay station in the middle
and a big shed that looked like it
was once an automatic car wash.

The gate at the entrance to
the petrol station was open and

hanging loosely on its hinges. But if we could somehow block that one gate, the area would be secure.

'THERE!' I said, pointing to the petrol station. 'We need to **LURE** them into there. Then we can contain them until we get help.'

'Sounds good, but how do we get them in there?' Zeke asked.

'I think there's only one way,' I said. **'AVATAR BAIT.'**

TUESDAY— ALMOST SUNSET

The **MORNING** of the zombies was getting louder and they were heading in the direction of the fence surrounding the compound. We had to lure them back towards the petrol station.

'Zeke, you're the fastest. You can outrun and outmanoeuvre a zombie, for sure,' I said.

Zeke nodded.

'Do you think you can get them to **CHASE** you into the petrol station?' Jez asked.

'Sure can,' Zeke said, doing a standing back somersault just to prove he was up to the task.

'Jez and I will go inside the petrol station fencing where the zombies can see us. Then, when they come inside, we'll **TRAP THEM** in there.'

'But, bruh, how are you both going to get out of there without touching them? If you touch them, you'll be contaminated,' Zeke said.

I swallowed hard. 'I guess we just have to be **FAST.'**

'In the meantime, keep an eye out for the boss zombie. I don't know what it will look like, but it's the key to rescuing Max,' Jez said.

Zeke and I nodded.

'BRAAAAAAINNNSSS!' the mob moaned, coming en masse towards the front of the compound.

'Let's go!' Zeke said.

TUESDAY— IN THE PETROL STATION

As we entered the abandoned petrol station, Jez found an old rusty pipe on the ground.

'This will be perfect to jam the gate shut once we get all the zombies in here,' she said.

'I'll go around to the back and get their attention. You hide behind the crates at the entrance, and

once they're all in, get out and
jam the gate closed behind you,'
I instructed.

'What about you?!' Jez protested.
'You'll be stuck in here with the
ZOMBIES!'

'I—I . . .' I stammered as I thought
about being locked in with a pack
of drooling zombies. 'I'll think of
something!' I said quickly. I'd have
to deal with it when the time came.

The zombie moans were deafening
now and I could see them all
limping up the street.

'Hey, you ugly green boogers! You can't **CATCH ME!**' Zeke yelled as he danced in front of the mob.

All at once, the zombies turned their wobbly heads towards Zeke. **'AVATAR BRAAAINS!'** one of them moaned.

Zeke ran up the street doing **BACKFLIPS** to keep their

attention. We needed them *all* interested in Zeke so that they would follow him.

The zombies gained speed as they pursued the smell of avatar brains. I was surprised at how fast they were—I thought zombies were slow and dragged their limbs behind them. But with the promise of an avatar dinner, they'd become a lot **FASTER** than I imagined they would be.

I jittered nervously. Maybe it wouldn't be as easy to outrun them as I'd thought.

'Jez, hide,' I called to her, watching the zombies get closer.

Jez hid behind the crates at the entrance to the petrol station, the metal rod in her hand, poised and ready to jam the gate shut.

Zeke was now running at **FULL SPEED** and the zombies were matching his pace. I could see the terror in his eyes as he realised that the zombies were almost as fast as him. We definitely weren't expecting that!

'Bruh, I'm bloxxed!' Zeke cried,

puffing. I saw the desperation in his eyes and the sweat on his block head.

'Hey, zombies! Want some avatar dinner?!' I yelled, waving my arms in the air.

The zombies looked past Zeke and saw me bouncing up and down inside the petrol station area.

Zeke did a **SOARING LEAP** to the front of the fence, then a massive side sault over the top, landing inside. Without Zeke to distract them, the zombies were now focused on the open gate before them and the tasty avatar bouncing around—me!

While the zombies were distracted, Zeke ran into the small hut, which would have once been the old pay station. I saw him burst into the open doorway and collapse on the floor, **PANTING** and trying to catch his breath.

Knowing Zeke was safe was a huge relief. I needed to make sure the zombies didn't go into the hut, so I continued to jump wildly and wave my arms.

One by one, the zombies stumbled through the open gate. There had to be at least twenty of them now and I **GULPED,** thinking about how I was going to outrun them all.

Once the last zombie had lurched inside, I quickly ducked behind a petrol pump to hide. I needed time to think, but they would sniff me out soon.

Jez quickly leaped up from behind the crates and closed the entrance gate. She **JAMMED** the metal pipe into the mesh fence, locking the gate. But she'd **LOCKED** herself inside! What was she doing?!

Jez scurried from the crates over to one of the petrol pumps, hiding behind it. She made sure none of the zombies were watching her before she ran to the next one and hid behind it too. Eventually, she got all the way to the hut where Zeke was hiding and slipped inside. Just before disappearing through the doorway, she gave me a **WINK** and a thumbs up.

Typical. Jez was such a loyal friend. There was no way she was going to leave Zeke and me alone to fight twenty zombies. I should have known she'd do that!

By this point, the zombies were running around in a **FRENZY,** looking for the cheeky avatar who had lured them inside. They limped to the far side of the petrol station, opposite from where the hut Zeke and Jez were hiding in. I took that as an opportunity to stealthily crawl into the hut too so I could make a plan with my friends.

'It's not going to take them long to find us in here,' Zeke said. He had caught his breath and was ready to go again.

'We need a plan,' I said in a shaky voice, 'to get to the boss zombie and then get out of here.'

We all rose up onto our knees and looked out of the hut window. I could see the tiny Max zombie **HUNTING** around for avatars.

'**LOOK!**' Jez gasped, pointing to the centre of the mob.

In the middle, protected by the throng, was a zombie that looked different. When he stood up straight, he was much larger than the others. He had the same green skin, but all around him was a hazy green **GLOW,** like fire.

'BOSS ZOMBIE, I bet,'
Zeke said.

Jez and I nodded.

'But how do we destroy him?'
I asked.

'I've read a bit about zombies
before,' Jez said. 'We can take
him down, but he won't die—
he's already dead after all. He'll
RESPAWN. But if we can
immobilise him, then the other
zombies will probably take him
back home to respawn. At least
that's what I think might happen.'

'It's worth a try,' I said.

'But how do you knock out
a zombie?!' Zeke asked.

We looked blankly at each other.
Then we heard a loud moan.

'AAAAAVVVVAAAATAAAARS!'

TUESDAY— SUNSET

We looked up and a zombie stood at the entrance to the hut. We'd been caught! And she was calling the other zombies over to us.

GULP!

'Throw something at her!' Jez said, picking up a stick from the ground and **HURLING** it at the zombie. But it bounced right off her and she didn't seem bothered whatsoever.

FAIL.

Zeke opened his backpack and
started rummaging for something
to throw. I reached in too, trying
to help. I yanked out the first
thing I touched—a bottle of
lemonade. I **THREW** it as
hard as I could at the zombie.
She didn't even flinch as it
bounced off the zombie's head.

The bottle rebounded onto the
ground and started spinning in
circles. I could see the bubbles
frothing up inside. Then suddenly,
the lid of the lemonade popped off,

sending a stream of fizzy
drink shooting out of the top.
The lemonade covered the zombie.

The zombie looked
down at the bubbly,
fizzy drink on her skin.
'FIIIZZZY!'
she moaned.

We looked at each other, confused.
Did zombies drink lemonade?

'Look!' Zeke said.

The zombie's skin began to
FIZZLE and then she

started to **MELT** before
our eyes!

'Fiiizzzy!' she yelled again.

After a few seconds, the zombie
was a soft heap of green goo.

'Is she gonna **RESPAWN?**'
I asked, remembering what Jez
had said earlier.

'Maybe,' Jez said. 'But that
would take time. We know what
they're allergic to, so now we have
a **WEAPON!**' she said, a smile
creeping across her face.

'Wait!' I said suddenly. I ripped
open Max's backpack, which
I was still holding from before.
Inside were the three **WATER
BLASTERS** he'd brought
along to the compound to fight
the monsters.

'Max's water blasters are going to
be useful after all!' Zeke beamed.

'Clever little guy,' Jez said quietly.

I pulled out the three water
blasters and gave one each to
Jez and Zeke. We unscrewed
the tanks and Zeke pulled out

his remaining bottles of lemonade.
One by one, we filled the water
blasters with the drink. It **FIZZLED**
and **POPPED** as we poured it in.
We screwed the tanks back into
place then stood up.

'Ready to kick some zombie butt?'
Zeke asked.

'Let's go!' I yelled.

TUESDAY— LATER

We stepped over the green pile of zombie goo and out into the darkening evening.

'Zeke, you go left, and Jez, you go right. I'll go up the middle,' I instructed. 'Once we reach the boss zombie, we'll all need to regroup to get him.'

Zeke peeled off to one side and Jez to the other.

'It's time for some **ZOMBIE MELTING!**' Zeke yelled as he sprayed the first zombie that approached him. The zombie stood, shocked, before it started to melt.

A second zombie waddled towards me and I lifted my water blaster. I pumped the tank and then pulled the trigger. It was just like a water fight at a pool party. A spray of clear, bubbling liquid came out, soaking the zombie in front of me.

'FIIIZZY!' he moaned as he melted.

I could then see the boss zombie **GLOWING** at the far end of the station. That's where we needed to go.

I ran and ducked behind a petrol pump. I could see a zombie approaching Jez, and she showered it with lemonade. But then another zombie sneaked up behind her.

'Jez, **LOOK OUT!**' I yelled, jumping out into the open. I sprayed the zombie hard and he melted into a soft heap just seconds before he would have grabbed Jez.

Phew! That was close.

'Thanks, Ari!' she called.

'Boss zombie, twelve o'clock,' Zeke
said, pointing straight ahead.

I nodded then **BLASTED**
another zombie with the fizzy
liquid. But then a mob of zombies
limped over to me. Five against
one? I didn't like my chances.

I pumped the chamber of the
water blaster as hard as I could.
Then I pulled the trigger and let
out a massive torrent of lemonade.

I sprayed them all, soaking them from head to toe. The zombies melted before my eyes until they were small piles of ragged clothes and soft zombie putty.

I ran straight up the middle of the petrol station until I reached the glowing **BOSS ZOMBIE.** As I approached, he stood to full height and turned to look at me. He was so much **BIGGER** than I'd anticipated and his skin glowed with green fire. His eyes were red and drool hung off his crooked brown teeth, dripping onto his shirt.

'AVATAAAR,' he snarled, reaching out towards me.

TUESDAY—
LATER STILL

'AAAAGGGH!' I screamed as
I pumped my water blaster. But
I could feel the tank was getting
lighter. The spray that came out
wasn't anywhere near as strong
as what it was before. I was
RUNNING OUT of liquid.

'Zeke, Jez!' I hollered. 'I need
BACKUP!'

Zeke and Jez ran over, pumping
their tanks. Then they pulled the

trigger. But their sprays were also getting weaker. Although the liquid hit the boss zombie, it fizzled on his skin only slightly before it dripped off.

'I think he needs **A LOT MORE** lemonade than the others!' Jez shrieked.

We continued to spray him with our water blasters, but there wasn't a lot of liquid coming out anymore.

'Cover me—I have **ONE BOTTLE LEFT!'** Zeke yelled as he opened his backpack.

The boss zombie saw his chance. We tried to distract him by continuing to soak him, but he'd seen Zeke crouch down. Moving at the speed of light, he leaped forward and grabbed Zeke. Zeke **DROPPED** the bottle of lemonade, which went rolling under a nearby crate.

'ZEKE! NO!' Jez shouted.

We looked on in horror as Zeke froze. His eyes rolled back in his head and his skin began to change colour. Slowly, his face and body turned green. His features became monstrous and his teeth turned brown.

Zeke was a **ZOMBIE!**

'Avaaaataaaaars,' he moaned, looking up at Jez and me.

'AAAAAAAGGGGGH!' we screamed.

'Don't blast Zeke,' I warned Jez. 'We don't know what it will do to him. We've gotta get the boss zombie!'

Jez continued to spray any zombie that came near her, all while running from Zombie-Zeke and the boss zombie.

I **RACED** over to the crate where the bottle had rolled and I ducked down. I could see it wedged between the crate and the wall.

With the other zombies chasing Jez, this was my chance. I lay down and reached as far as I could. My fingers touched the bottle, but I couldn't get a hold of it.

I looked up, checking that no zombies were approaching me. But what I saw was much worse. It was the boss zombie! He'd seen me! He stopped chasing Jez and began racing **TOWARDS ME,** knowing that I was vulnerable on the ground.

'AVVATAAAR!' he moaned.

My fingers slipped around the lemonade bottle, unable to properly grasp it. The boss zombie was coming at me, **FAST.**

With one last shove, I pushed my

arm in as deep as I could under the crate. Sharp splinters pierced my skin as it scraped the wood, and I gritted my teeth against the pain. But my hand finally closed around the lemonade bottle.

'Ari! He's coming!' Jez cried in horror.

I **YANKED** the bottle out as hard as I could. I **SHOOK** up the bottle with all my might, then pointed it directly at the boss zombie, who was rushing towards me like a terrifying freight train.

'Nobody **ZOMBIFIES** my friend!'
I yelled, unscrewing the lid and
aimed it right at his menacing,
glowing face.

The lemonade shot out of the bottle with force. It **BLASTED** the boss zombie's face with such speed that it sent him stumbling backwards. He lifted a dead arm to his eyes to try to wipe off the liquid. But the lemonade was doing its job. I kept spraying until the bottle was completely **EMPTY.**

Now there was no lemonade left. None in the bottle. None in my water blaster.

This had to work.

The boss zombie shook his head

violently from side to side. He
moaned in anger as his face
started to crumble.

It was **WORKING!**

Finally, his head and body melted
to the ground in a soft pile of
flaming goo. The rest of the
zombie mob froze.

The **FLAMES** from the
boss zombie's goo shot outwards,
connecting with each of the
zombies around us. One hit
Zombie-Zeke, and another flame
connected with a little zombie in

a black baseball cap—Zombie-Max.

'**NOOO!**' Jez screamed, terrified
that her friend and brother were
hit with fire.

But as the flame hit them, the
green on their skin **MELTED**
off like paint in the shower.
Underneath, Zeke and Max's
normal avatar skin was revealed.
Their faces went back to normal,
and their teeth returned to their
usual white colour.

'**MAX!**' Jez yelled, running over
to her little brother.

'JEZ!' he yelled back.

Jez enveloped Max in an **EPIC HUG** as she laughed and cried at the same time.

'You saved me!' Max said. 'Why?'

'Why?!' Jez cried disbelievingly. 'Because you're my little brother!'

'But I thought you didn't like me,' Max said softly.

Jez's face relaxed into a warm smile. 'Max, I love you. We're family, and even though you can be totally annoying sometimes, I will always have your back. We're a **TEAM,** Max!'

In that moment, I thought about my sister, Ally. For some reason, I would have given anything to be at home with her, eating popcorn and watching our favourite movie together.

'Whoa, that was . . . **WEIRD,'** Zeke said as he shook his head.

'You're back!' I **WHOOPED,** pulling him into a hug.

'Bossssss!' a nearby zombie groaned, looking at his leader in a pile of putty on the floor. He gathered him up.

'RESPAAAAWWN,'

he moaned.

All the zombies that were still standing gathered up their melted comrades from the floor. Then they limped towards the petrol station's gate. 'Should we let them out?' I asked.

'They want to go back home through the **PORTAL**,' Jez said. 'I think we're safe now.'

She ran over to the gate and pulled out the metal rod. The gate swung open and the remaining zombies limped out, carrying the goopy green piles of their **MELTED** friends.

We kept our distance, but followed them back through the compound to make sure they were heading to their portal.

'I feel kinda bad for them,' Zeke

said, watching them go through the portal one by one.

'We didn't actually *kill* the boss zombie. Zombies don't die. They'll respawn on the other side. And in the meantime, this portal will close,' Jez said. 'If you ask me, I'd much rather zombies stay in a different dimension to mine.'

'That's for sure,' I added.

The **LAST** zombie popped through the portal and we all **EXHALED** in relief.

'When will the portal close?'
I asked Jez.

'According to my calculations, it should close within the next hour. I don't think they'll be able to respawn and come out in that time,' she said, smiling.

'PHEW!' I said. 'What a ride. And to think that we were only able to blox those zombies because of you, Max!' I said, turning towards the little avatar.

Max was holding Jez's hand tightly. **'REALLY?'** he asked

with wide eyes.

'Yep, we used your water blasters
to fry them. You're a **HERO,'**
Zeke added.

Max looked up at Jez and she
nodded in agreement. 'Yep, you
sure are, little bro,' she said. 'And
you too, Ari,' she added, looking at
me. 'Turning them into lemonade
blasters was all your idea.'

I smiled.

Jez crouched down so Max could
jump onto her back. She stood up,

carrying him like a backpack.
'Ready to go, **BUDDY?**'
she said.

'Let's get out of here!' Max yelled.

SATURDAY MORNING

I knocked lightly on Jez's front door. Zeke stood next to me, bouncing with impatience.

Jez opened the door and her mum stood behind her.

'Hi, avatars,' Jez's mum said.

'Hi!' Zeke and I chorused.

'Where are you all going today?' she asked.

'We're going to ride our **SKATEBOARDS** to the park, if that's OK?' Jez said.

'All good. Just be back for lunch,' Jez's mum said.

'Can I come too?' a little voice piped up from behind Jez.

It was Max, his eyes wide and full of hope.

'Oh, Maxy, Jez is skateboarding with her friends. Why don't you and I watch a movie instead?' Jez's mum suggested.

Max looked sad.

'It's OK, he can come with us,' Jez said. 'If that's OK with you avatars?' she said to Zeke and me.

'Sure thing.'

'No problem!'

'REALLY?!' Max said, his eyes lighting up.

'Yeah, grab your helmet and your bike. You can come to the park and play on the equipment while we do some stunts,' Jez said.

'**WOW!**' Max beamed as he ran towards the garage to get his bike.

'That's real nice of you, Jez,' Zeke said, as we walked down the driveway.

'Well, I guess he's not too bad,' Jez said, shrugging. 'Better than . . . I dunno . . . a **ZOMBIE BROTHER!**'

We all laughed. As we waited for Max, I saw a figure on a bike approach from the distance. Pink streamers tossed about in the wind as it came closer.

'HEY, ALLY!' I said,
recognising my sister.

'I'm just riding to the store, I'm not
following you,' she said.

'No, **WAIT!'** I called after her.
She stopped on her bike and
turned towards me. Her mouth
was tight, like she was waiting
for me to say something mean
to her. I thought about Max in
the compound. 'We're going to the
park. Max is coming too. Do you
want to come?'

Ally froze and then narrowed her

eyes, unsure if I was messing with her. 'For real?' she asked.

'For real,' I said with a nod.

Ally's eyes **LIT UP** and she smiled brightly.

'Ready!' Max called, riding his bike out onto the driveway.

'Let's go!' Jez yelled, jumping onto her skateboard.

As we all rode to the park, I breathed in the warm air.

'RACE YOU, MAX!'

Ally hollered as she stood up on her pedals.

Friends are great. But I guess family is pretty great too.

ALSO AVAILABLE: